March 2010

Preaching—With Integrity

D1764762

Andrew Moore

Regent's Park College, University of Oxford

GROVE BOOKS LIMITED
RIDLEY HALL RD CAMBRIDGE CB3 9HU

Contents

To the memory of Canon Dennis Moore

The cover image is copyright © David Cannings-Bushell

First Impression October 2012
ISSN 1470-854X
ISBN 978 1 85174 843 3

How Can We Preach About *God* with Integrity?

1

Some months ago I was asked, 'How can we preach about God with integrity today?' I am not certain what my friend had in mind—he is a Christian—but it is a question worth pondering.[1]

We can approach it in three ways. How can we preach about *God* with integrity? In a post-Christian culture, deeply imbued with militant secularism and scornful atheism, what kind of fool would expose himself or herself to ridicule by standing up and holding forth on such an apparently irrelevant and outmoded topic as God? Then, how can we *preach* about God with integrity? Preaching has a bad image, it is tainted and suspect; in vernacular English, 'preaching' is cognate with ranting. The only **The media pay attention to preachers who promote religious hatred or have been caught in some scandal** preachers the media pay attention to are those who are alleged to promote religious hatred or who have been caught in some, usually sexual, scandal. So, next, how can *we*—morally compromised as even the best of us are—preach about God with integrity? How can we human beings presume to preach, to instruct and direct others in the things of a holy God? In what follows we shall take these questions in turn.

Who is the God Whom Christians Preach?

Many voices in our culture claim to speak about, and on behalf of, God. Christian voices no longer dominate the conversation, so we face a question about preaching and the identity of God. Who is the God whom Christians preach? Non-believers are not without reason if they feel confused. For example, there are Muslim voices: some seem reasonable, open- and generous-hearted; others, anything but. And then there is syncretism: pick-and-mix religion that takes the Golden Rule from Christianity, reincarnation from Hinduism, adds some tree hugging and inveighs against organized religion. (To mistake this manifestation of religion for the Church of England is a forgivable sin.) Nor must we forget the secular humanists who preach against God but who seem not to be too clear on who this God is whom they denounce. '[Richard] Dawkins's God is…a repulsive superego,' observes Terry Eagleton in his review of Dawkins's *The God Delusion*.[2] Is this the God Christians preach?

And as if non-Christian voices did not already add up to a cacophony of confusion about the identity of God, the church itself speaks with an unclear voice. Some seem to the general public to preach a God of love who could not, and even if he wanted to, would not, say 'Boo' to a goose; others seem to preach a vengeful God of hate—a sinister, hovering vulture of a deity. So how do we preach about *God* with integrity? Who is this God we preach; what kind of God is he/she/it; and how might we faithfully convey the reality of the God of Christian faith?

It would be easy to think that the answer to these questions is straightforward: the God who uniquely revealed himself in Jesus Christ. Of course I am going to argue that that is the correct answer, but the problem is that the God of Jesus Christ gets mistaken for other deities—and that not only by non-Christians and ill-informed Christians but by preachers too. The first commandment is sufficient reason for taking scrupulous care to avoid misidentifying or confusing with other deities the God in whose name alone we are saved. We may not have Ba'al worshippers today, but we live in a polytheistic world, and the unique identity of the God of the gospel can be conflated with others, even in a Christian pulpit.[3]

The God of the Philosophers

What (or perhaps, who) are these other deities? The God of the gospel of prosperity, of health and the pursuit of happiness, is an obvious example—though currently perhaps less attractive with the failure (for the time being) of the God of *laissez-faire* capitalism. But there is a less immediately evident candidate whose way into the pulpit is more subtle because cloaked with apparently greater intellectual respectability. I am thinking of the God in whom Blaise Pascal did *not* find 'Certainty, certainty, heartfelt, joy, peace'—the God of the philosophers.[4] Here, to get ahead of myself, insecurity about our calling as preachers can produce confusion about the identity of the God we are called to preach.

A variety of Gods who exist as the termini of chains of reasoning

Nowadays there is a variety of philosophers' Gods—Gods who exist as the termini of chains of reasoning. The most bare-faced of these is the impersonal, deist God who made the whole show, lit the blue touch-paper, set the mechanism running and is now alive and well but working elsewhere on a less ambitious project. This is the God to which the design argument infers and in whose existence the well-known former atheist Antony Flew came to believe a few years back: '…a God very different from the God of the Christian,' he says, '…there is no room for any supernatural revelation of that God or for any transactions between that God and individual human beings.'[5] How do you preach about that kind of God? What compelling reasons are there to get excited about, to wish to tell others about, a God who is not and even if he/she/it could, would not wish to be involved in the mess, muddle and confusion of human life, still less to change it? This is a God who, even if he/she/it wanted to, could not become incarnate and bear away our sins at Calvary.[6] There is little, if any, good news to be told about this God.

Or there is the God of theism—who also is the terminus of an argument. According to philosophers such as Richard Swinburne, this deity represents 'the core Western doctrine of God': a personal God who is involved in his creation but to whom different faiths add different bolt-on extras. Each of Judaism, Christianity and Islam is a species of theism having the same core features (being personal, omnipotent, omniscient, simple and so on) but with different additions—giving the Torah to the Hebrews; becoming incarnate in Jesus Christ; or having Mohammed as his Messenger, for example. This deity is frequently encountered as the terminus of proofs in works of contemporary philosophy of religion by such well-known Christian apologists as Richard Swinburne and Alvin Plantinga; 'he' also haunts the pages of popular works of Christian apologetics.[7] There are a number of attractions to taking the theistic God of the philosophers as the God who is the subject of Christian preaching. For example, the powerful arguments in favour of 'his' existence lend the pulpit some academic legitimacy and cloak its occupier in intellectual respectability. It is not unusual for this God to make an appearance in sermons on apologetics and one Trinity Sunday I even once heard an Anglican bishop proclaim a God strikingly similar to this.[8]

Is this God of the philosophers identical with the God of Paul?

But is this God identical with the God of Paul who, in the cross of Christ, has 'made foolish the wisdom of the world'? And who, 'since, in the wisdom of God, the world did not know God through wisdom, God decided through the foolishness of our proclamation, to save those who believe'? (1 Cor 1.20f). Paul was clear about both the uniqueness of the God of Jesus Christ and the dangers of idolatry. So, since our polytheistic culture is in many ways relevantly similar to that which Paul addressed in 1 Corinthians, it seems to me that the onus of proof is on the preacher tempted to blur the boundaries between Christian theology and theistic philosophy to establish that the God of the philosophers is indeed the God of the gospel.

The preacher of the God of the philosophers might reply against Paul that in our circumstances of religious plurality it is advantageous to advocate belief in a personal God whilst being non-committal on issues that divide different religious traditions.[9] If so, the following challenges will need to be met. What the philosopher might regard as 'additions' to a core doctrine of God are not so easily separable from the content of preaching. For example, with what interpretative gloss might someone committed to preaching the God of theism interpret 1 Corinthians 1.17 ('For Christ did not send me to baptize but to proclaim *the* gospel') or Romans 10.9 and 17 ('…if you confess with your lips that *Jesus* is Lord and believe in your heart that God raised him from the dead, you will be saved…[F]aith comes from what is heard, and what is heard comes through the word of *Christ'*)? And how is Paul's Christocentric understanding of preaching to be rendered coherent with a Muslim's focus on the Qur'an and Mohammed? Nor in practice do most believers put their faith in the God of generic theism; they put their faith in the God of their particular religious tradition. (Ask yourself, 'How many professing theists do I know?') Even the God of *Christian* theism is a philosopher's abstraction; some would even go so far as to call it an idol.[10] Although advocates of Christian theism are clear on the need for revelation and grace, there are very substantial philosophical and theological problems to be overcome before we can be clear that the God who revealed himself in Jesus Christ is the God of the philosophers. So until proof of the identify of the God of the gospel and the God of the philosophers is forthcoming, prudence suggests we retain our theological integrity, avoid philosophical blandishments and resolve 'to know nothing among [those to whom we minister] except Jesus Christ and him crucified' (1 Cor 2.2).[11]

These misidentifications of the God of the gospel are made under the influence of the challenges that modernity and its outworkings in the Enlightenment posed to Christian faith. In face of these cultural pressures, some say that the task of the preacher is to make the church's teaching believable, to make the gospel consistent with what scientific knowledge of the world tells us is true and real. It is just this accommodation and its fruits that I am urging we reject.

The God of Romanticism

Science has indeed been a major influence on what we take to be real and what we consider the best way to arrive at knowledge of it, but there is another factor. Science is only one product of modernity;[12] it emphasized detached, cool, neutral reason but the Enlightenment generated its own counter-movement.

Romanticism generated the God who is experienced in our consciousness of a 'feeling of absolute dependence'

By contrast with Enlightenment rationalism, Romanticism was all about feeling and passion rather than intellect and calculation. And just as scientific modernity produced the Gods of deism and theism, so Romanticism generated the God whose defining characteristic—according to the greatest theologian of the period, Schleiermacher—is that he is experienced in our consciousness of a 'feeling of absolute dependence.' God is the 'source' of this feeling.[13]

The Catholic political philosopher Charles Taylor seems to me right when, in his recent book *A Secular Age*, he argues that Romantic expressivism has bequeathed to us our current age of authenticity, characterized as it is by 'the understanding of life…that each one of us has his/her own way of realizing our humanity, and that it is important to find and live out one's own.'[14] Christians are not immune to the attractions of this culture of self-actualization: I choose to attend a church in which I feel comfortable, where I can associate with the kind of people I desire to identify with, which offers me the kind of spiritual development I feel (based perhaps on a book of popular psychology) suits my needs, and which gives me the kind of emotional high I associate with God's being powerfully present.[15] '[A] powerful emotional response to God's saving action was more important than theological correctness': Taylor's judgement concerns eighteenth-century Pietists and Methodists who inadvertently helped prepare the ground for Romanticism but it is equally applicable to much contemporary Christianity. '[T]hese movements,' he continues, 'wished to remain within orthodoxy, but it would not be long before the emphasis will shift more and more towards the strength and genuineness of the feelings, rather than the nature of their object.' It is not necessary to spend long in some contemporary British churches to have a sense that little has changed since the period of which Taylor is writing. Now, as then, the underlying conviction seems to be that '[o]ne can only connect with God through passion. For those who feel this, the intensity of the passion becomes a major virtue, well worth some lack of accuracy in theological formulation.'[16,17] Of course there are differences between then and now, but it seems to me that the emphasis on our affections in contemporary Christian worship, and a focus on existential fulfilment rather than matters of doctrine in preaching, is eloquent witness to our being members of the age of authenticity.

One question to ask here is, 'Who is God for us today?' For example, we might profess that God is our highest good. But what *is* our highest good? Is it what *we* think and desire? If so, how do we obtain that which *God* offers? Is it through emotionally satisfying worship and preaching that emulate self-help manuals? Well, perhaps it is—if we are content to name ourselves Narcissus and think that God is but a higher, better, more fulfilled, more fully realized version of ourselves. For according to the gospel, human authenticity is arrived at only

Human authenticity is arrived at only by forsaking all that one considers essential to authentic life

by forsaking all that one considers essential to authentic life; and the God of the gospel is God incarnate, not merely a man of highly developed God-consciousness who differs from other humans only in degree.[18] So the age of authenticity risks presenting us with 'authenticity' at the cost of losing that human 'fulfilment' which is only found through death and rebirth in Christ.

The God of Judgment and Grace

The problem with both Rationalist and Romantic traditions is that neither allows sufficiently, if at all, for that abyss which is spanned only by the arms of the crucified Christ: the abyss of sin that separates God and humanity. Each recognizes that a bridge—whether of reason or of feeling—must be built and each can give a place for faith and grace, but neither acknowledges the fact that sin places an absolute gulf, unbridgeable in principle by human beings, between us and God.[19] Neither gives sufficient weight to the fact that the word of God spoken in Jesus Christ is a word both of judgment against human self-sufficiency and an act of grace that restores the sinner to fellowship with God.

Augustine is sometimes cited as a thinker who reconciled the claims of contemporary philosophy (Platonism in his case) and its vision of the human good with Christianity, and as the one whose work laid the foundations for modern understandings of the self. But in neither the Rationalist nor the Romantic traditions do we find the sense of human incapacity and need for grace that we find in, for example, Augustine's celebrated confession:

> Late have I loved you, beauty so ancient and so new,
> late have I loved you!
> Lo, you were within,
> but I outside, seeking there for you,
> and upon the shapely things you have made I rushed headlong,
> I, misshapen.
> You were with me, but I was not with you.[20]

For Augustine—just as for those who would walk in the paths of the great preachers—it was when we were dead in our sins that God made us alive in Christ. How then can we preach about *God*? By preaching not impostor deities invented by philosophy and the spirit of the age, but the God who, in the mercy of his love, assumed human flesh, has graciously called us to fellowship with himself, and has given us his Spirit to perfect us and lead us into the truth about himself.

How Can We *Preach* About God with Integrity?

2

This question raises the obvious further question, What is preaching? In answering it, I take my direction from Romans 10.17—*ara hē pistis ex akouēs, hē de akoē dia rhēmatos Christou* ('So faith comes from what is heard, and what is heard comes through the word of Christ').[21] Cranfield (and others) interprets the genitive in the last phrase as subjective: 'Faith comes through Christ's speaking the message by the mouths of his messengers.'[22] This understanding of preaching is confirmed by 1 Peter 4.11: *ei tis lalei, hōs logia theou* ('Whoever speaks must do so as one speaking the very words of God'). J N D Kelly takes *lalei* here to refer to 'teaching and preaching.'[23] Likewise Cranfield, who comments:

> Does someone preach? If what he does is really preaching, then it is no human accomplishment, but a miracle. Preaching is God's Word. But the only words that the preacher can utter are human words, all of them broken and inadequate. Preaching only takes place when the Holy Spirit works a miracle and makes them become a real witness to the Word of God, themselves a living Word of God to the hearers. This is something which no preacher can 'lay on' or produce at will. He is dependent on the free decision of God.[24]

Cranfield here stands four-square in the tradition of Calvin who, in the *Institutes*, writes that:

> Those who think the authority of the Word is dragged down by the baseness of the men called to preach disclose their own ungratefulness. For, among the many excellent gifts with which God has adorned the human race, it is a singular privilege that he deigns to consecrate to himself the mouths and tongues of men in order that his voice may resound in them.[25]

In other words, we misunderstand preaching if we think of it as primarily a human activity; rather, it is God's action by which he sets human beings apart to serve him in this holy office so that his word of judgment and grace may be spoken and heard with the obedience of faith.[26]

God addressed himself to us archetypically in his Word incarnate; in Christ he has overcome our deafness and enabled us to hear him; by his Spirit he has borne witness to himself in the church through appointed human agents. This means that the emphasis in preaching is not on the act of preaching or on the content of words uttered but rather on the declaration of an event: *ho logos gar ho tou staurou...dunamis theou estin* (1 Cor 1.18, 'For the message about the cross...is the power of God').[27] On being declared by the preacher, the event effectually declares itself afresh. We can only trust God for that. It is no human eloquence that renders preaching the power of God; indeed, skill and artifice may be suspect lest they declare only themselves.[28] It is no human declaration, no matter how well-meaning, of any human message of justice, peace, and inclusion—such as the United Nations Universal Declaration of Human Rights—that effects God's work. Of course, this does not mean that it does not matter how we comport ourselves in the pulpit or what we take as the content of our preaching. Preaching should be 'logic on fire,' as Martyn Lloyd Jones memorably put it. Preaching should expound Holy Scripture: it is there (uniquely) that God's saving

> **Preaching is the declaration of the word of God as it is attested in Holy Scripture**

action in Christ is attested; to take anything else as the content of preaching would be to empty the cross of its power. The epitome of preaching is the declaration of the crucifixion, resurrection and ascension of Jesus Christ in which God has reordered and restored his lost, fallen and sinful creature. So, since the Christ-event is the culmination of God's saving acts narrated in the Bible, we may infer that, more broadly speaking, preaching is the declaration of the Word of God as it is attested in Holy Scripture.[29] These definitions are offered as theological statements; they are not drawn directly from Scripture or presented as exegesis of it and, similarly, the practice of preaching cannot be accomplished by parroting the Bible: it is the free declaration of God's act of setting humanity free.

Freedom to Preach

Preaching, then, has integrity when it is obedient to the task of declaring God's deed in Jesus Christ. I mentioned in my introduction the poor image that surrounds preaching. But that need not overly concern us—so long as it is *Christian* preaching. The integrity of preaching evidences itself in the way in which God's Word effects that which it promises, and that is from faith to faith by the work of the Holy Spirit. Thus, although ours is an age whose only goal seems to be personal authenticity and whose sole ethical principle seems to be autonomy, although—in other words—our age repudiates authority that it has not chosen for itself, this will not stifle or inhibit Christian preaching which declares that freedom for which Christ has set us free. Likewise, we might feel embarrassed by the image of preaching, but the integrity of Christian preaching is not impugned by those whom the media term 'preachers' but who preach hatred. Or are we ashamed of the gospel of Jesus Christ? For in declaring the cross of Christ, preaching declares God's judgment against that sin which separates us from him and from one another, and that love by which he binds all things into one. The media may tar all preachers with the same brush but Christian obedience requires that Christ is proclaimed—or else how shall the world hear the good news? So we need not enter the pulpit anxious lest our hearers close their ears because our society scorns preaching, nor when there should we expend energy offering apologias for preaching: 'God chose what is foolish in the world…' (1 Cor 1.27).

The Rhetorical Stance of the Preacher

The content of preaching is self-authenticating and needs no human defence (if such a thing were possible), but there remains a difficulty, and this concerns what we might call the rhetorical stance of the preacher. What position *vis-à-vis* their hearers does the preacher occupy? Is it, for example, like that of salesmen or advertisers wishing to convince their hearers of the superiority of their product to that of their competitors? We might be tempted to answer that it is: the gospel of Jesus Christ is being declared to an audience which needs to be persuaded that it should 'buy' him in preference to the Gods of the money market, of the shopping precinct, of the self-help manual, of New Age superstition, and so on. This temptation is to be resisted. The God of the gospel is not a God amongst equal and competing Gods—they have been nullified. The content of the gospel is incommensurable with that of God's supposed competitors and, in a similar way, so is the means by which it is marketed: it is by the folly of preaching that God conveys his 'product.' So the rhetorical stance of preachers standing before their congregation should not be compared to any other; their office is unique.

The Enlightenment Stance

To bring this out further we may consider another aspect of the question. The age of authenticity is, as we have seen, an offspring of the Enlightenment; both aim to promote human autonomy. As Kant famously puts it in his 'What is Enlightenment?':

> Enlightenment is man's release from his self-incurred tutelage. Tutelage is man's inability to make use of his understanding without direction from another. Self-incurred is this tutelage when its cause lies not in lack of reason but in lack of resolution and courage to use it without

direction from another. *Sapere aude.* 'Have courage to use your own reason!'—that is the motto of enlightenment.[30]

The Enlightenment ideal is that reason is used critically upon all authority—all 'direction from another'—whether Aristotle's, the Pope's or the Bible's. On this account we should only accept for belief that which can be legitimated by reason and evidence. This is a commonplace of educated opinion, whether in a newspaper leader or the university lecture room. Such has been the power of this view that its acceptance within Protestant Christianity in the West is almost universal, whether in Liberal or Conservative wings of the church.[31] 'Without direction from another': this implies that if there is any place for preachers in the church, their rhetorical stance should be one of coolly neutral detachment. They should present the gospel as a matter for free rational decision on the basis of evidence and argument lest they compromise both it and their hearers' autonomy.

But this view of the preacher's rhetorical stance denies the transcendence of Christ and hence the real basis of human freedom. In his lectures on *Christology*, Dietrich Bonhoeffer writes that, 'The object of our study [that is, Jesus Christ] can only be shown to us again in the proclamation itself.' He continues:

[Christology] has no proof by which it can demonstrate the transcendence of its subject. Its statement that this transcendence, namely the *Logos*, is a human person, is presupposition and not subject to proof. The transcendence which we make the subject of proof instead of letting it be the presupposition of our thought, is no more than the immanence of reason which comes to grips with itself.[32]

That which we can prove by evidence or reason is that whose nature we can bring within our control and use as an instrument of a human project. To preach the gospel of Jesus Christ as something that could (*per impossibile*) be the object of evidential or rational proof might flatter us, but it would (again, *per impossibile*) deny the freedom of God whereby he has set us free from the grip of sin and death. Along with the whole fallen person, reason which had once been curved in upon itself is set free by the loving authority of God's Word and enabled to offer to God that 'rational worship' by which alone humans are transformed out of conformity to this world.[33] In other words, for the preacher to adopt the cool 'reason and evidence' stance of the lecture room or of the newspaper leader would be to give the impression that the gospel is something within the scope of human mastery when it is just this illusion that God has mercifully dispelled in Christ.

An illustration. It was Eastertide and the preacher's text was 1 Corinthians 15.12-19. First he presented evidence and arguments for the view that the most plausible explanation of what the New Testament says is that Jesus was indeed risen from the dead. He then went on to talk of the transforming, liberty-giving aliveness of Jesus. Whereas the first half of the sermon was intended to convince the minds of the more sceptical members of the congregation, the second was meant to appeal to their hearts. After the service an agnostic took the preacher by the arm and said, 'That was a great sermon but you know, it was far better when you told us about the aliveness of Jesus *now*—that was far more convincing than all the arguments you presented.'

The agnostic was right. In the first half of the sermon, the preacher had adopted the wrong rhetorical stance. The substance of the gospel of the resurrection is not arguments for empty tombs nor is it conveyed by them. Preaching the resurrection is not accomplished by informing pardoned sinners about the status of women as witnesses in first-century Palestine or practices of tomb veneration. To do this is to risk allowing our hearers to infer that there is some argument we must master, some evidence we need to grasp if we are to know the transforming power of the risen Christ; it is to imply that the preacher is amongst their congregation as one who possesses superior knowledge and who can use it to see off Christianity's critics. But that is to deny grace, to deny the power of God, and tacitly to seek to subject his authority to that of the court of secular opinion. The substance of the gospel is Jesus Christ, and its power that of the unique, living Lord; the miracle of the resurrection occurs every time God takes a preacher's words, makes them his own, and uses them for his purposes. What had persuaded the agnostic was the sense, whether its source was acknowledged or not, of the aliveness of Christ through the preaching.

The Stance of the Politician

One other possible rhetorical stance the preacher might seek to emulate is that of the politician. The successful politician is often a powerful orator. Whilst there is a place for soaring oratory in the pulpit (would that there were more!), those gifted in this way might remember that 'Christ did not send [Paul]... with eloquent wisdom, so that the cross of Christ might not be emptied of its power.' Paul did not come amongst the Corinthians with 'lofty words,' and it seems that they were not blind to his unimpressive personal presence—some even said, '"His letters are weighty and strong, but his bodily presence is weak, and his speech contemptible."' Not a model of rhetorical brilliance, then. Yet this allowed another kind of brilliance to shine forth. Though he himself, like all believers, is but a clay jar, this fragile, eminently disposable vessel contains treasure: 'The God who said, "Let light shine out of darkness"...has shone in our hearts to give the light of the knowledge of the glory of God in the face of Jesus Christ.'[34] Commenting on the Corinthian correspondence, Jerome Murphy-O'Connor OP writes that:

> The church is not a set of ideas which inform the mind, but a context of divine power which transforms the personality. Authentic ministers, in consequence, do not use their rhetorical training to develop persuasive arguments, but manifest the presence of the grace-giving Spirit. Faith is not the conclusion of a logical discourse, but is born of a vision of God at work here and now (1 Cor 2.1–5). Ministers assume the responsibility of being the place where the divine is active; their comportment must be such as to reveal the power of grace. They have to be able to say, 'Imitate me!' (1 Cor 4.17; 11.1).[35]

How Can *We* Preach About God with Integrity?

3

'Imitate me!' How many times have those words been preached on? Not many, I suspect. And the reason barely needs stating; the question of the integrity of the preacher is all too clearly in view. We are only too aware of how our own lives fail to measure up to our own moral standards, let alone those set by Paul—even if he was, as Murphy-O'Connor suggests, sometimes irascible and occasionally downright 'abusive.'[36]

Preachers need no reminders of this, but our integrity as people matters and it matters to us as *preachers* because we do not wish to be hypocrites who preach one thing but practise another. There are a number of other ways in which the question of our integrity can present challenges to us. For example, despite the fact that we believe the gospel and know that God has found us in Christ and that we are learning to live by faith in him, when we are honest with ourselves we know that we stumble and grope around in the dark to know more clearly this God whom we are called to proclaim. This, it seems to me, is an experience that authentically reflects that of the psalmist who wrote:

> Hear, O Lord, when I cry aloud, be gracious to me and answer me!
>   'Come,' my heart says, 'seek his face!'
> Your face, Lord, do I seek.
>   Do not hide your face from me.[37]

We face, that is, the question of our intellectual integrity.

And when we look at ourselves, how can we, frail morally compromised human beings, preach about God? One of my theological college tutors (a much-loved and well-respected preacher) wrote to me recently as follows, 'My response to God's gracious goodness towards me is ever a turbulent one, a boorish and traitorous kicking against the pricks, and the church of which I am a member is always re-enacting "Judas, one of the twelve."'[38] Again, if we subject ourselves to serious self-scrutiny, we know that though my teacher speaks with his own voice, he speaks a grim truth of our own hearts. We face the question of our moral integrity.

I will come back to this question shortly, but before doing so, I want to examine a different but important topic, for the questions I have just raised are embraced by a broader set of issues. Perhaps I can introduce it like this: How can we who are locked into our own finite, sinful perspective on the world presume to proclaim something that is universally true and of saving relevance to all humanity? How can we, with our unavoidably restricted knowledge, seek to proclaim a God who is not a possible object of our unaided experience? This is a metaphysical and epistemological malaise; it is that of relativism. Our pluralist culture in which there are many proposed claimants to deity has its impact on our moral and intellectual lives by making us relativists. 'God is in heaven and you are on earth, so let your words be few.' For many of us—and if not for us, then for our more thoughtful hearers—this text from Ecclesiastes (5.2) might summarize our worries about how a creature can proclaim their creator with integrity.[39]

The Universality of Jesus

It is tempting to think we can skirt these difficulties by appeal to the claim that the Bible is revelation and that therefore it is God's timelessly true word for all cultures. Although there is some truth in this, to accept it simplistically would be to ignore the hermeneutical question of how those words written in the thens and theres of the Bible are to be understood and proclaimed in our nows and heres. More damagingly, it would be to ascribe to the Bible powers and capacities that properly belong only to the one to whom it bears witness: *Jesus Christ* is the living Word, *he* is true life, *he* is the living and true way to the Father, *he* has been raised to the right hand of the Father's glory, and *his* Spirit has been poured out. It is this scandalous particularity of Jesus Christ in which lies his (and, derivatively, the Bible's) universality and it is that which gives us a clue how we can navigate the shoals of relativism.

It is Jesus' being a fully human person of the first century that undergirds his universal significance. As Rowan Williams and Richard Bauckham put it, '[o]ur suggestion is that Jesus transcends his particularity in the only way an individual can transcend his particularity without losing it: in his relationships. Jesus' universal relevance is to be found in his relationships, as a particular individual, to God and to other human beings.' This statement would be ascribing far too much to Jesus were it not for the fact that he was God incarnate, that he related to God in total obedience and that in him we see how God relates to human beings, and hence to us and our hearers. Thus,

[t]he universal significance of Jesus is to be found *in* his specific historical identify, not despite it or outside it. If Jesus is abstracted from his particular history, made into some generalized notion of ideal humanity or divine presence, Everyman or God-Man or God-in-Everyman, if he becomes interchangeably Jew or Gentile, black or white, male or

female, ancient or modern, then paradoxically *his* universal significance evaporates.[40]

But because Jesus is alive now as ascended and glorified Lord, he is able, by his Spirit, to communicate the Father's presence to any person alive now.

So, appealing to the Bible as God's timelessly true revelation can be of help only if we remember that it points us to Jesus Christ as God's living Word.[41] It is his living presence which makes what the Bible says about him capable of leading people to him now. It is not the concepts that the Bible puts into currency which make it capable of conveying salvation today; it is not the Bible, theology, Christianity or the church that is the unique way to the Father. It is Christ. '[R]emember, I am with you always' (Matt 28.20).

Interpretative Agnosticism

A related point: it is very hard to put our theology to one side when we prepare to preach, but if we do not we put the integrity of our preaching at risk by speaking more of ourselves and our own ideas than of Christ, and then we are back in the mire of relativism. But if we really accept the authority of Scripture, all our ideas should be tested by it and subjected to its normative role. If, on the other hand, we think ourselves capable of understanding the Bible from our own perspective, we risk making the Bible the servant of our own theology and then, once again, we are trapped by the limitations of our own perspective. To avoid this, it can be helpful to enter into a prayerful, expectant, interpretative agnosticism in which we suspend what we think we know in order to become docile and understand what the Lord wishes to disclose through his Word now.[42]

Dietrich Bonhoeffer describes the kind of ascesis I have in mind in a letter about biblical interpretation written in

God meets us through the Bible but we must 'allow God to determine the place where he will be found'

1936. He is emphatic that God meets us through the Bible but he emphasizes that in reading it we must 'allow God to determine the place where he will be found,' otherwise, if 'I determine the place in which I will find God...I will always find there a God who in some way corresponds to me.' The danger here is of evading—as we are wont to do—'the very place in which God has decided to meet us...the cross of Christ.'[43] This stance exemplifies how radical the *sola scriptura* principle is. For Bonhoeffer, to presume to understand what God wishes to say through anything other than his Word—through the lens of a theology or a church tradition, for example—is impossible. He simply asks of each passage, 'What is God saying to us here?'[44] To bring into interpretative consideration '[a]ny place outside the Bible has become too uncertain for me. I fear that I will only discover some divine double of myself there.'[45]

The cost of allowing God to address us through the Bible, of allowing him to question us through it, is the highest there could be for anyone who values their own intellectual integrity. But denial of self is the first condition of discipleship. As we shall see shortly, we should not cling to our integrity, for—as Bonhoeffer goes on—the cost is, 'just in these matters, and only in these matters, with respect to the one, true God,' a *sacrificium intellectus*.'[46] Bonhoeffer has attended to that word of God which, in Second Isaiah (I have in mind those passages in the Servant Songs where God humbles his hearers by defying them to prove that he is God, to know his ways, or to accomplish his purposes), requires a similar *sacrificium intellectus* of his people.[47] For as William Cowper also learned—albeit in a different context—'God is his own interpreter.'

So whilst all preachers are children of their own time and place, if they are seeking to proclaim Christ as he is attested by Scripture, if they are seeking to empty themselves of themselves and their own theologies and ideas, then their words uttered in God's name will not be empty. It follows that preachers should not attempt or pretend to be otherwise than who they are in their own local and historical contexts lest they wish to preach a (supposedly) timelessly true philosophy. Rather, to know the word of Christ for our own context, we need to be thoroughly immersed in it, just as the Word incarnate was in his.[48] We do not possess a perspective-transcendent perspective on life and nor are we called to. We are called to proclaim 'not ourselves' but one who was 'crucified also for us under Pontius Pilate…suffered and was buried, and the third day…rose again…and ascended into heaven.'

If integrity means exemplifying one's own principles in one's own conduct, then Paul's score was off the scale: he lived an exemplary life of righteousness, not just according to his own, his society's, or his religion's principles but according to God's, yet all this he counts as refuse, excrement. To rank his integrity on this scale would have been to put 'confidence in the flesh.' What mattered to Paul was righteousness but 'that comes through faith in Christ' (Phil 3.6, 4, 9). Similarly for us, it is not integrity that ought to be our primary concern but righteousness.

We can be too precious about integrity.[49] Not only does righteousness matter more, but worrying about our integrity draws our attention to ourselves rather than to Christ. When we examine ourselves and assess our moral successes and failures, is our attention on him? If it is, then we know that we are forgiven and free to serve him; if it is not, then sin and blindness threaten. Integrity may indeed be the state of being true to ourselves, but the truth of who we really are is not known to us. In Colossians, Christians are instructed as follows:

> Set your minds on things that are above, not on things that are on earth, for you have died, and your life is hidden with Christ in God. When Christ who is your life is revealed, then you also will be revealed with him in glory. (Col 3.2–4)

The gospel can be seen as a quite definite injunction *not* to be ourselves; that is, the one the flesh instructs us we are is who we are not. Paul teaches that in our baptism we have become who we *really* are: we have clothed ourselves with Christ.[50] Integrity is found in so looking to Christ that we become that person—the redeemed one, clothed in an alien righteousness. So it need not concern us whether we think we do know or whether we know that we do not know who we really—this particular, individual person with these unique gifts, this temperament, these capacities and incapacities, those strengths and vulnerabilities. *Christian* personal integrity is found when we '[p]ut to death… whatever in [us] is earthly' and 'put on the Lord Jesus Christ, and make no provision for the flesh' (Col 3.5; Rom 13.14).

This applies to all Christians, not just preachers, but, in particular, those who are called to proclaim the word of Christ should strive to be able to say with Paul, 'I have been crucified with Christ; and it is no longer I who live, but it is Christ who lives in me' (Gal 2.20). Not that this is a state in which Paul thought he, or any other mortal, could be said to have arrived whilst living 'in the flesh'; it was something that lay ahead of him.[51] He has, as all preachers should, a holy 'fear that after having preached to others I myself might be rejected.' In other words, he is, as Héring puts it, fully aware of 'the general principle that one who does not practice what he preaches will have no permanent success.'[52]

The thought of preaching on St Paul's injunction to 'Imitate me!' makes us squirm. But Paul had his rough edges (and he seems to have been aware of them, too), so the injunction needs to be read as a sign of God's mercy and of the transcendent power of the glory of Christ which shines through the earthen vessel of human vulnerability. Recoil from our vulnerability is rejection of the sufficiency of grace—in which case, we have plenty of reason to avoid preaching on the phrase. On the other hand, the preacher has integrity when what they practise and what they preach is the righteousness of Christ.

4

Conclusion

A preacher who fails to practise what they preach is rightly viewed as a hypocrite—which is partly why the vocation to preach can seem onerous. But it follows from what we have just seen about our identity in Christ that, humanly speaking, hypocrisy is unavoidable for all Christians. Without prayerfully seeking the Holy Spirit's assistance we can neither live up to our profession on human terms—unless we have exceptionally low standards—nor on God's terms. And whether or not that assistance is conspicuously evident in our lives, the appearance of hypocrisy is our lot. But that is not the end of our story; indeed, it is a distortion to regard preaching in this way. Preaching takes place in a broader context which sets what I have been arguing in a fuller and more proper perspective.

The first context is our authorization as ministers of the gospel when we were ordained or licensed; it is in virtue of the church's discernment that the Lord has called us to be preachers that we dare enter the pulpit. To dispel from us any sense that it is owing to any capacity of our own or any learning we may possess that we may preach, in our ordination the bishop gives us a Bible and says, 'Receive this book, as a sign of the authority given you this day to speak God's word to his people.'

The next, and principal, context is that of the sermon itself. Some readers will have noticed what to them will be an obvious and hence curious omission from my argument so far. I have not mentioned the Holy Communion—the exemplification of our need to go on being converted and incorporated into the living Word who is our righteousness. Here, in the liturgy of Word and sacrament, what Pascal referred to as the *'grandeur et misère'* of the human condition—of the preacher's condition—is shown forth, precisely as the infinitely greater reality of the death of Christ for our sins and his being raised for our justification is revealed.[53] We are both 'unworthy to gather up the crumbs from under [the Lord's] table' and also 'made clean by his body and...washed through his most precious blood.' 'Lord, to whom can we go? You have the words of eternal life' (John 6.68).

Recommended Reading

Karl Barth, *Homiletics* (Louisville: Westminster/John Knox Press, 1991)

Dietrich Bonhoeffer, *Discipleship* (Minneapolis: Fortress Press, 2001)

Ruth Burrows, *To Believe in Jesus* (London: Sheed and Ward, 1978)

C E B Cranfield, *The Bible and the Christian Life* (Edinburgh: T and T Clark, 1985)

Oliver O'Donovan, *The Word in Small Boats* (Grand Rapids: Eerdmans, 2009)

John Webster, *Holiness* (London: SCM, 2003)

John Webster, *The Grace of Truth* (Farmington Hills: Oil Lamp Books, 2011)

Rowan Williams, *Open to Judgement: Sermons and Addresses* (London: Darton, Longman and Todd, 1994)

William H Willimon, *Conversations with Barth on Preaching* (Nashville: Abingdon Press, 2006)

Notes

1   A remotely related, earlier version of this paper was given to groups of clergy and LLMs in Chichester and Oxford dioceses. I am grateful for the comments offered.

2   In the *London Review of Books* (19 October 2006; available online at http://www.lrb.co.uk/v28/n20/eagl01_.html). Eagleton illustrates other of our themes when he says in the same article that 'Dawkins, it appears, has sometimes been told by theologians that he sets up straw men only to bowl them over, a charge he rebuts in this book; but if *The God Delusion* is anything to go by, they are absolutely right. As far as theology goes, Dawkins has an enormous amount in common with Ian Paisley and American TV evangelists. Both parties agree pretty much on what religion is; it is just that Dawkins rejects it while Oral Roberts and his unctuous tribe grow fat on it.'

3   On the identity of the God of the gospel, see Robert Jenson, *Systematic Theology, Vol 1: The Triune God* (New York: Oxford University Press, 1997) pp 42–60.

4   Blaise Pascal, *Pensées* (London: Penguin Classics, 1995; A J Krailsheimer (trans)) p 285.

5   The quotations are from an Associated Press news report <http://abcnews.go.com/US/wireStory?id=315976> and an interview published in the Winter 2005 issue of *Philosophia Christi* <http://www.biola.edu/antonyflew/flew-interview.pdf>

6   For more on this, see my 'Who are the Liberals now?': History, Science, and Christology in N T Wright and Alister McGrath' in *Anvil* 20/1, 2003, pp 9–24.

7   See, for example, Richard Swinburne, *The Coherence of Theism* (Oxford: Clarendon Press, 1977) p 1 and *The Christian God* (Oxford: Clarendon Press, 1994) pp 1–3; Alvin Plantinga, *Warranted Christian Belief* (Oxford: Oxford University Press, 2000) p 1 and *cf* pp 349–350. The quotation is from Swinburne, *The Christian God*, p 2.

8   The sermon went something like this: the arguments for God's existence show that it is rational to believe in a God, but this God can seem remote from us; Christian believe that God assumed humanity in Jesus; he is God with us; but how do we link God up there to God with us? That is the role of the Holy Spirit. At least the preacher had three points.

9   Perhaps the most eloquent defence of pluralism is John Hick, *An Interpretation of Religion: Human Responses to the Transcendent* (Basingstoke: Macmillan, 1989); for an equally eloquent rebuttal, see Gavin D'Costa, 'The Impossibility of a Pluralist View of Religion' in *Religious Studies* 32 (1996), pp 223–232.

10 See Walter Kasper, *The God of Jesus Christ* (London: SCM, 1983), pp 294–295 and my *Realism and Christian Faith* (Cambridge: Cambridge University Press, 2003) pp 21–39.

11 If I may be permitted an autobiographical anecdote, a principal reason for my taking the direction I have in my publications is that I found that I could not preach a theology shaped by the tradition of Christian theism I had once sought to defend. Barth is correct: 'Theology as a church discipline ought in all its branches to be

nothing other than sermon preparation in the broadest sense' (Karl Barth, *Homiletics* (Louisville: Westminster/John Knox Press, 1991) p 17).

12 And, in many ways, a massively beneficial one.

13 Friedrich Schleiermacher, *The Christian Faith* (Edinburgh: T and T Clark, 1928; H R Mackintosh and J S Stewart *et al* (trans)) §4.3-4, p 16. It is salutary to note that Karl Barth could say both that 'I can see no way from Schleiermacher...to the God of Abraham, Isaac, and Jacob and the Father of Jesus Christ' and that Schleiermacher 'had a personal relationship with Jesus which might well be characterized as love' (Karl Barth, *The Theology of Schleiermacher* (Grand Rapids: Eerdmans, 1982) pp 271–272, 274).

14 Charles Taylor, *A Secular Age* (Harvard: Harvard University Press, 2007) p 475.

15 *A Secular Age*, p 486.

16 *A Secular Age*, pp 488, 489.

17 One might argue that the dissent of some conservative churches towards moves to ordain non-celibate gays suggests that we do in fact care about accuracy in theological formulation. But against this, we may place the theological shallowness of many dissenting theological formulations (and also many of those in favour).

18 Recall Barth's words about Schleiermacher: 'One can *not* speak of God simply by speaking of man in a loud voice,' *The Word of God and the Word of Man* (London: Hodder and Stoughton, 1928) p 196.

19 Thomas Aquinas is the source of many theistic arguments but, influenced as he was by Aristotle, he—in common with his contemporary successors—underplayed the fallenness of the human intellect. See Peter Harrison, *The Fall of Man and the Foundations of Science* (Cambridge: Cambridge University Press, 2007) p 43ff. (This is not to say that Thomas himself would have endorsed this philosophical use of his work.) The case of Romanticism is more complex, but since Schleiermacher presumes a Christian piety and adopts a phenomenological approach to Christian life it is perhaps not surprising that he understands sin more in psychological than theological terms.

20 *Confessions* (London: Hodder and Stoughton, 1997; Maria Boulding, OSB (trans)) X.27.38. For more explicit acknowledgement of the indispensability of the grace of Christ in his conversion from philosophy, see *Confessions* VII.20.26.

21 *cf* Luke 10.16.

22 C E B Cranfield, *The Epistle to the Romans, Vol II* (Edinburgh: T and T Clark, 1979) p 537.

23 *A Commentary on the Epistles of Peter and Jude* (London: A and C Black, 1969) p 180. He comments, 'What the Christian spokesman enunciates, if he is faithful, is God's word; he does not simply repeat the divine message, but God speaks through him' (*ibid*).

24 *The First Epistle of Peter* (London: SCM, 1950) p 98.

25 John Calvin, *Institutes of the Christian Religion* (Philadelphia: The Westminster Press, 1960; John T McNeill (ed), Ford Lewis Battles(trans)) IV.1.5. In a footnote to the passage quoted, the editor notes that '[t]he ministers of the "the heavenly doctrine" [IV.1.5] speak with God's own voice; *cf* Calvin's *Homilies on I Samuel* xlii,

where the prophets and pastors of the Christian church are said to be "the very mouth of God"...' Calvin carefully circumscribes the authority of preachers: they are 'to teach what is provided and sealed in the Holy Scriptures...faithful ministers are now not permitted to coin any new doctrine, but...are simply to cleave to that doctrine to which God has subjected all men without exception' (IV.8.9).

26 For OT precedents, recall Isaiah 6; Jer 1.1–10; Ezek 1.28c–3.11.

27 Paul's description of his own preaching and presence in Corinth (1 Cor 2.1–5) bears witness to just this kind of action of the free grace of God when his deed in Christ is proclaimed.

28 *cf* 1 Cor 2.4f.

29 The New Testament distinguishes between 'preaching' and 'teaching.' In some authors—for example, the Luke of Acts—commentators do not detect a difference of meaning; in others—for example, Matthew and the Paul of Colossians—commentators do. It seems to me that, whilst 'preaching' may rightly include 'teaching,' the latter is not a substitute for the former.

30 Immanuel Kant, 'What is Enlightenment?' in *On History* (New York: Macmillan Publishers, 1985; Lewis White Beck (ed)) p 3.

31 For more on this, see my 'Who are the Liberals Now?' (Note 6 above).

32 Dietrich Bonhoeffer, *Christology* (London: Collins, 1978) pp 27, 28.

33 Rom 12.1–2.

34 1 Cor 1.17; 2.1; 2 Cor 10.10; 4.6–7.

35 Jerome Murphy-O'Connor OP, *Paul: A Critical Life* (Oxford: Clarendon Press, 1996) p 284.

36 The term comes from an index entry on p 414 of Murphy-O'Connor's *Paul* and refers to Paul's language in Phil. 3.2 which it is hard to see as less than insulting.

37 Ps 27.7–9; *cf* Augustine, *De Trinitate*, XV.2.

38 Quoted with permission.

39 The false Gods we looked at in the first section can be seen as attempts to overcome the problem; so too, in a different way, can the mistaken rhetorical stances we examined in the second.

40 Richard Bauckham and Rowan Williams, 'Jesus—God with Us' in Christina Baxter (ed), *Stepping Stones* (London: Hodder and Stoughton, 1987) pp 24, 23.

41 *cf* John 5.37ff.

42 The argument I am presenting is not to deny that we ought to test our reading of the Bible theologically. This is vital, but our theology should conform to the Bible, not *vice versa*.

43 Dietrich Bonhoeffer, *Meditating on the Word* (Cambridge, MA: Cowley Publications, 1986; David McI Gracie (ed and trans)) p 44–45.

44 *ibid*, p 45.

45 *ibid*, p 46. The value of using the readings appointed in the lectionary is obvious.

46 *ibid*, p 46.

47 *cf* Job 42.1–6. Calvin generalizes the point: 'We are not our own: in so far as we can, let us therefore forget ourselves and all that is ours. Conversely, we are God's: let us therefore live for him and die for him...O, how much has that man profited who, having been taught that he is not his own, has taken away dominion and rule from his own reason that he may yield it to God!' *Institutes*, III.7.1.

48 It follows that for the sake of the gospel, clergy ought not to be shut up in their studies and busy in the sanctuary but engaged with the lives of their parishioners.

49 *aphthoria* which NRSV renders as 'integrity' does not occur in the LXX and in the NT only at Titus 2.7 ('in your teaching show integrity'), where etymology suggests it has the sense of uncorruptness.

50 Gal 3.27; the active verb here should be read alongside the passives of Rom 6.3ff.

51 *cf* Phil 2.21ff; 3.12ff.

52 Jean Héring's comment—in his *The First Epistle of St Paul to the Corinthians* (London: Epworth Press, 1962) p 83—on 1 Cor. 9.27, his own translation of which was quoted in the previous sentence.

53 Calvin seems to have thought that 'no meeting of the church should take place without the word, prayers, partaking of the supper, and almsgiving' (*Institutes*, IV.17.44; *cf* IV.17.39 and 46).